MW01154818

A *Stormy Tales* Production

- In loving memory of Stormy Weather, from whom I learned so much, and with special gratitude toward my parents, who never questioned why I brought animals home from the street, and never turned any of them out, leading me to a life of rescue. To my generous, brilliant, inimitable father, for his always unconditional love, unwavering support and constant belief in my talents, and for gifting me his laughter as he read this book in spite of the pain that afflicted him in the end. And to my husband, my children and all the animals who, with inmense patience, have taught me that we should suspend judgement on the intelligence of other beings.

- A. Abella

Original Title: *Stormy Says: Let´s Talk! A kids' guide to understanding dogs*
Title in Spanish: *Stormy Dice: ¡Hablemos! Una guía infantil sobre perros*
Copyright © 2014 by Alejandra Abella, StormyTales
Author and Illustrator: Alejandra Abella
Art Direction: Richard Sanchez Design

ISBN-13: 978-1506197579
ISBN-10: 1506197574

FIRST EDITION.

Stormy Says: Let's Talk!

A kids' guide to understanding dogs

Stormy says: Let's talk!

Is this how dogs chat? Noooo!
We can't use words like humans do but
we can still be friends.

We use our faces, and
our bodies, and our
sounds to communicate.

Let's see how ...

Stormy says: Be happy!

I use my tail to show I'm happy.

The happier I am,
the faster it wags!

Stormy says: Let's play!

Here's my formal invitation:
It's called a play bow!

stormy says:
Let's play chase!

Stormy says: Let's be friends!

We doggies smell each other's behinds to find out almost everythng there is to know.

"Are you from this neighborhood?"

"What did you eat today?"

What?... Isn't that how everybody introduces themselves?

Stormy Says: Sometimes I don't
want to be friends!

I show my teeth
and growl.

Grrrr.....

Or I get stiff and turn my head away.

And then I turn my head back as a warning: I need some space here!

But don't be sad because I'm mad;
I'll be glad again later!

How do you act when you are mad?
And doesn't it always
get better?

Stormy says: Let's make up.

I lick my friends just like my mommy licked me when I was a puppy. That made me feel good.

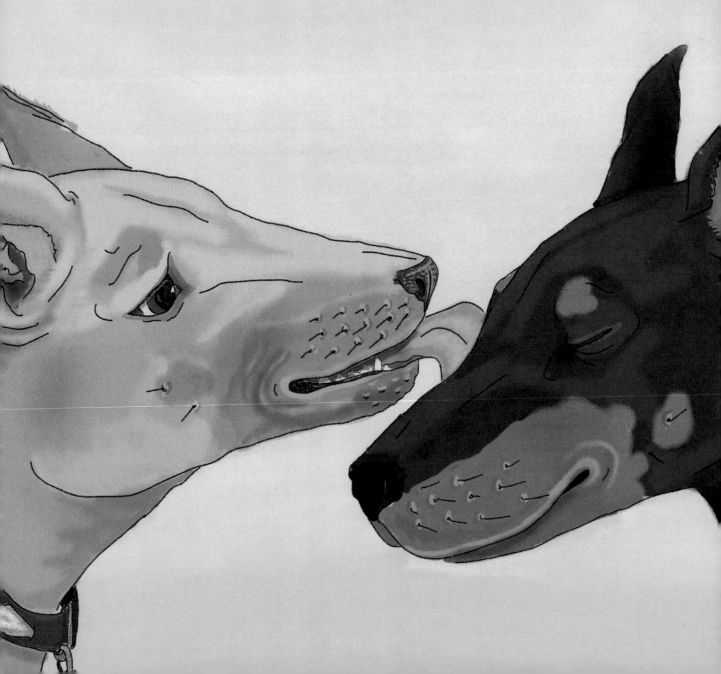

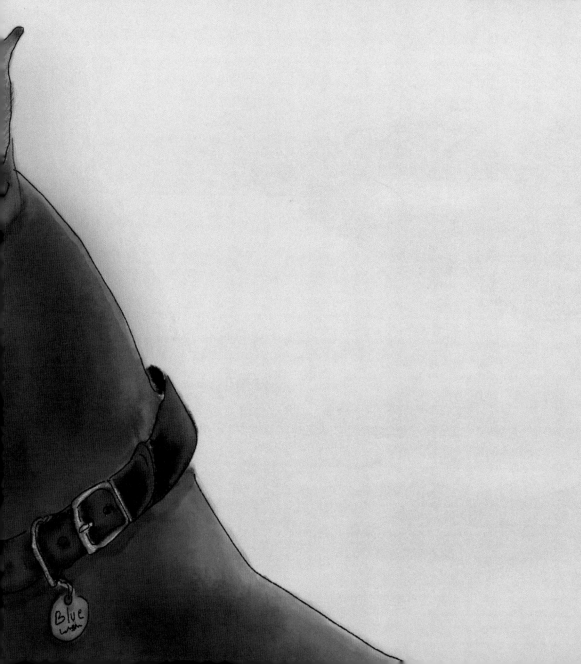

How do you make things better,
small Human?

Stormy says:

I'm worried, I'm sad.

Do you think this is
how doggies
show concern?

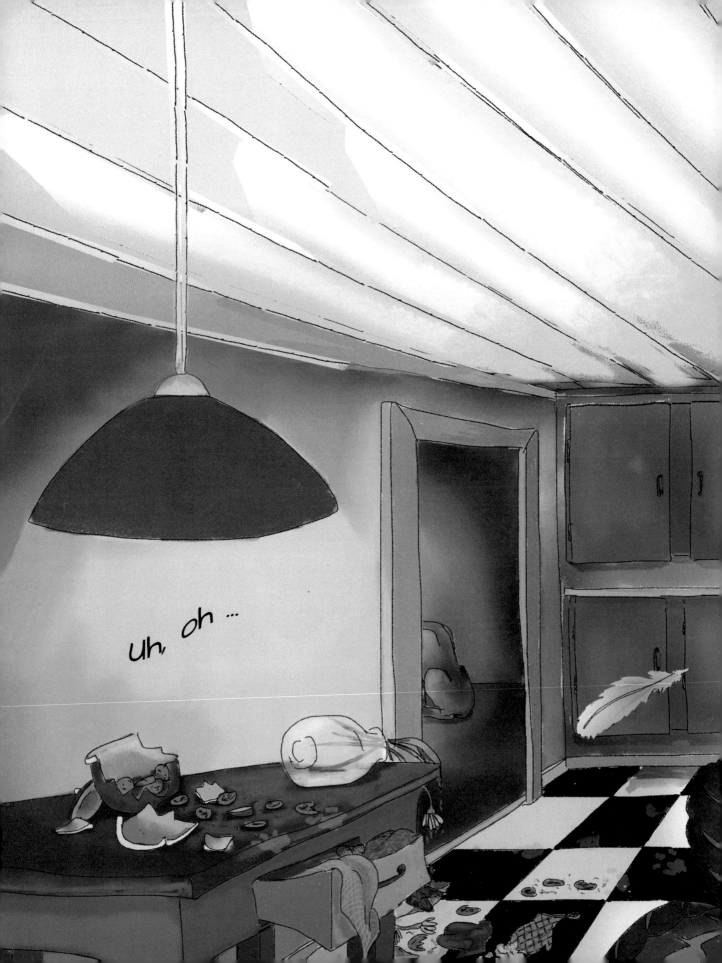

Stormy says: Are you still mad?

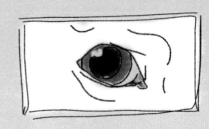

I look up ...

I look down ...

Hmmm ... I'll stay down here until I'm sure.

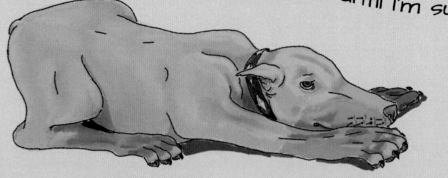

Stormy says: Rub my belly, please.

It's my softest side
so I'm trusting you not
to hurt me.

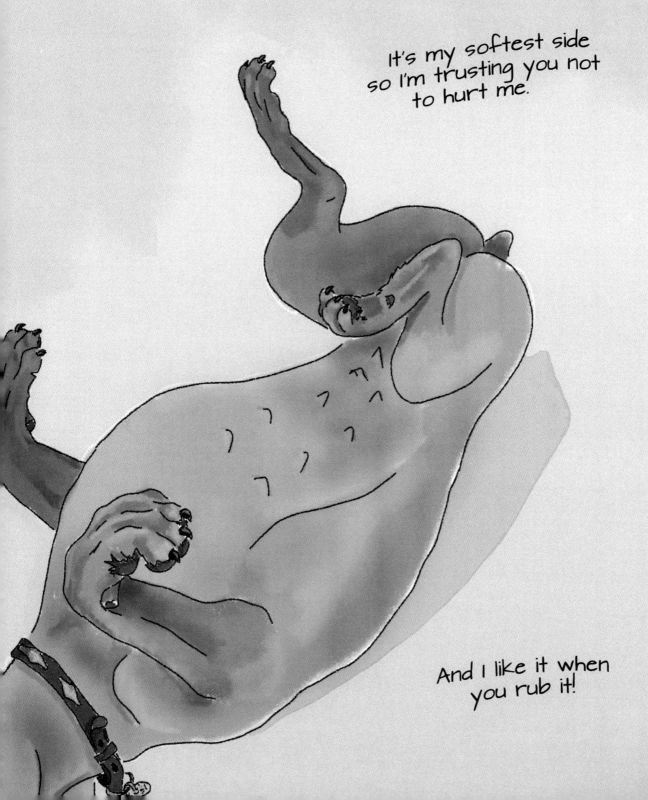

And I like it when
you rub it!

Stormy Says: Sometimes I try to "smile"
like a human.

I squint my eyes, and curl up my lip, and
show my teeth but I'm not mad!

Not every dog can do this special "smile"
and I do it to please you!

Everybody likes a smile!

Stormy says: Feed me!

But I don't like to share my food and my things!

Do you know how doggies protect their stuff?

Sometimes we guard our things with our paws or our mouths.

It's best to let us eat alone.

Is this how doggies go to the bathroom?

... and twist and turn and pace ...

... and bark at the door!

Stormy says: Any friends out there?

Woooooo ...

Whooooo...

Whooo...

Whooo, ooo!

Wiiiooo, wiiiioooo!

woo, wawawoo!

Awooo, wooo, awooo!

wi, wawiii, wi!

Wo, wo...

Do you howl too
when you want to see your friends?

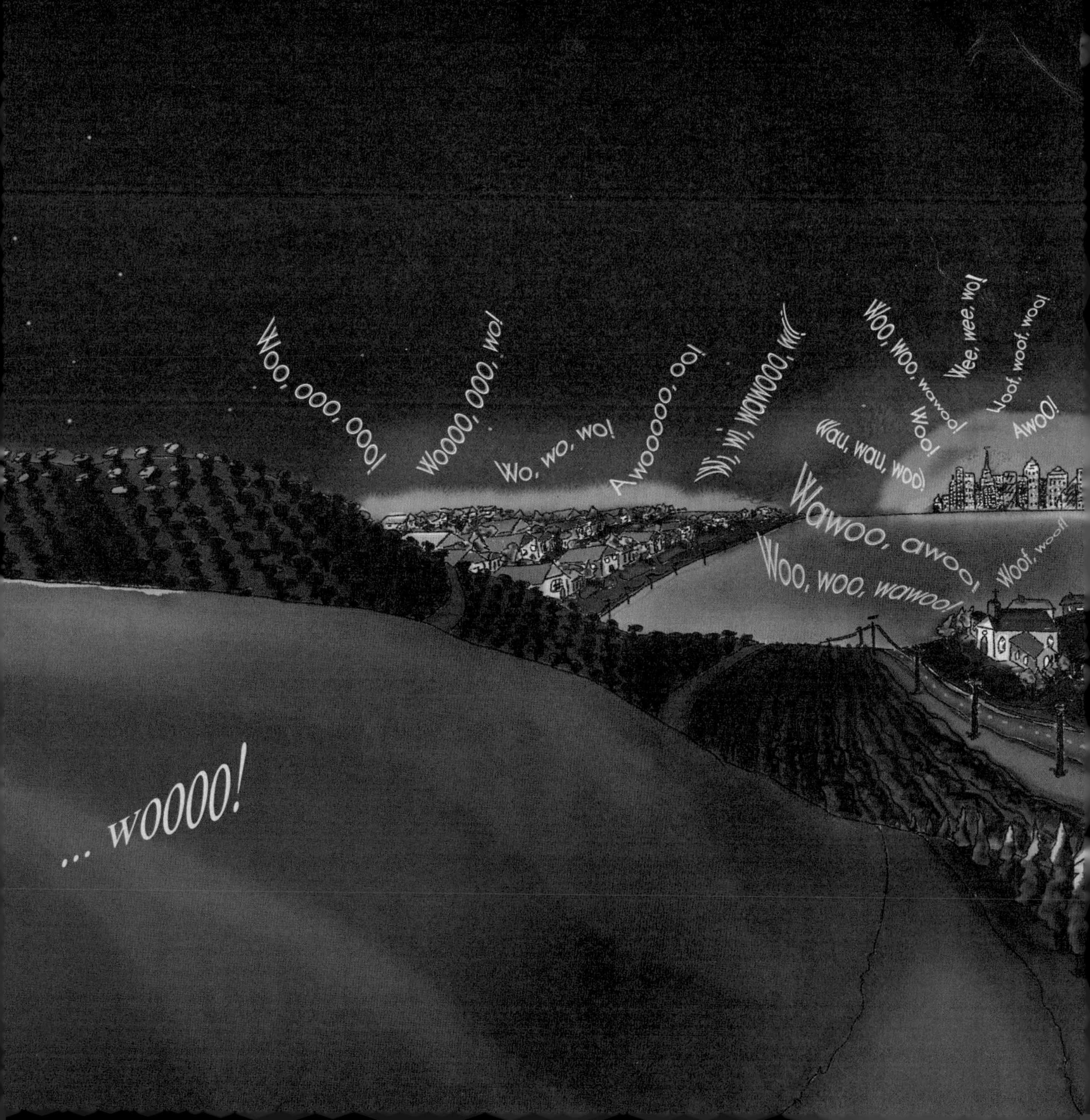

Stormy says: Time to sleep.

We lie off our hips so we can relax

How do you say good night?...

So what *IS* Stormy Saying on the cover?

Come sniff our website to post your answers, comments or dog stories, and to learn more about Stormy Tales adventures, books and promotions.

www.stormytales.com

Made in the USA
Middletown, DE
15 February 2021